Searchlight BOOKS™

What Is a Food Web?

Ocean Food Webs
in Action

Paul Fleisher

Lerner Publications Company
Minneapolis

Lerner Publications Company
A division of Lerner Publishing Group, Inc.
241 First Avenue North
Minneapolis, MN 55401 U.S.A.

Website address: www.lernerbooks.com

Library of Congress Cataloging-in-Publication Data

Fleisher, Paul.
    Ocean food webs in action / by Paul Fleisher.
       p.   cm. — (Searchlight books™—what is a food web?)
    Includes index.
    ISBN 978–1–4677–1255–2 (lib. bdg. : alk. paper)
    ISBN 978–1–4677–1777–9 (eBook)
    1. Marine ecology—Juvenile literature. 2. Marine plants—Juvenile literature.
  3. Marine animals—Juvenile literature. I. Title.
    QH541.5.S3F54 2014
    577.7—dc23   2012034177

Manufactured in the United States of America
1 – BP – 7/15/13

Contents

AN OCEAN FOOD WEB

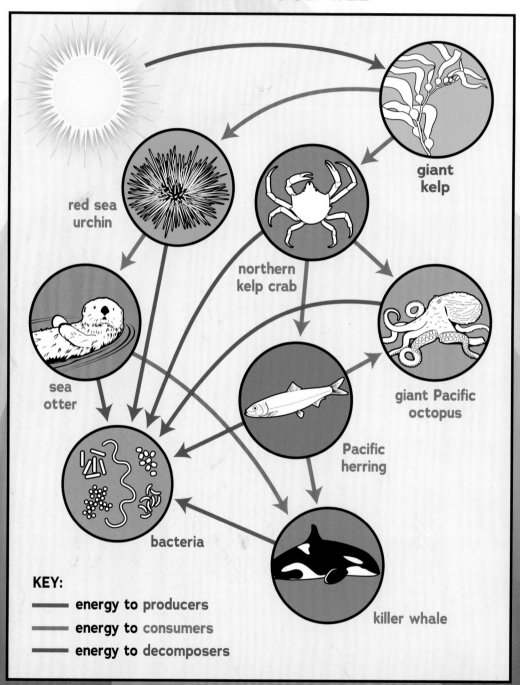

giant kelp

red sea urchin

northern kelp crab

sea otter

Pacific herring

giant Pacific octopus

bacteria

killer whale

KEY:
— energy to producers
— energy to consumers
— energy to decomposers

Chapter 1

THE OCEAN

From space, our world looks mostly blue. Look at a globe. Most of the globe is blue. Blue means water. We call our planet Earth. Maybe we should call it Ocean.

Almost three-fourths of the world is covered with ocean.

Most water on Earth is ocean water. Ocean water is salty. It is too salty to drink. But it is full of life.

This is how Earth looks from space. The green parts are land. What are the blue areas?

A hawksbill turtle eats a jellyfish in the ocean.

Creatures in the Ocean

Creatures of all sizes live in the ocean. Some are tiny. They are too small to see. Some are very big. Whales live in the ocean. They are the biggest animals on Earth.

Fish swim in the ocean. Worms burrow in the mud of the ocean floor. Clams live in the mud too. Crabs crawl along the bottom. Seabirds fly above the water. Many creatures live along the shore.

The ocean is a very important environment. An environment is the place where any creature lives. The ocean environment includes air, water, sand or mud, and weather, as well as plants and animals.

EARTH'S OCEANS

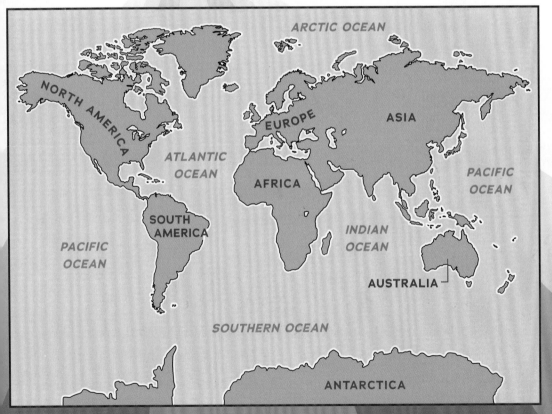

There are five oceans on Earth.

Food and Energy

Living things in the ocean environment depend on one another. They form a web of life. Some animals eat plants. Other animals are meat eaters. Some creatures feed on dead plants and animals. When plants and animals die, they break down into chemicals. The chemicals help other plants grow.

Fin whales and seabirds feed on fish called herring. The herring feed on tiny ocean plants and animals.

Turban snails get energy from food they scrape off kelp.

Living things get energy from food. Energy moves from one living thing to another. A food chain shows how the energy moves. The energy for life comes from the sun. The sun's energy is stored in plants. Animals eat the plants. They get some of the sun's energy from the plants. The energy moves along the food chain. When one creature eats another, some of the energy is passed on.

Food Chains

There are many food chains in the ocean. Here is one example. A snail eats plants. Then a fish eats the snail. Then a seal eats the fish. When the seal dies, crabs eat its body. Some of the sun's energy goes from the plants to the snail. Then energy is passed to the fish. Then energy goes to the seal. Crabs get energy from the dead seal.

THIS HARBOR SEAL
CAUGHT A FISH.

A food web is made of many food chains. Fish eat other things besides snails. They eat clams. They also eat worms and other fish. Seals eat many different kinds of fish. They eat octopuses and squid too. Crabs feed on all kinds of dead animals and plants. Everything each creature eats is part of a food web. A food web shows how all living things in an environment depend on one another for food.

This gull has found a dead fish to eat.

Chapter 2

OCEAN PLANTS

Green plants use sunlight to make food. Living things that make their own food are called producers. Animals use the food plants produce. Plants also make oxygen. Oxygen is a gas in the air and water. Animals need oxygen to breathe.

Sunlight shines through a giant kelp forest. Kelp and other ocean plants use sunlight to make food. What else do they make?

Making Food and Oxygen

Plants make food and oxygen through photosynthesis. Plants need sunlight for photosynthesis. They also need carbon dioxide and water. Carbon dioxide is a gas in the air. It is in the water too. Plants take in carbon dioxide. They take in water. Plants use energy from sunlight to turn water and carbon dioxide into sugar and starch. Sugar and starch are the plants' food. Plants store the food in their bodies.

HOW PHOTOSYNTHESIS WORKS

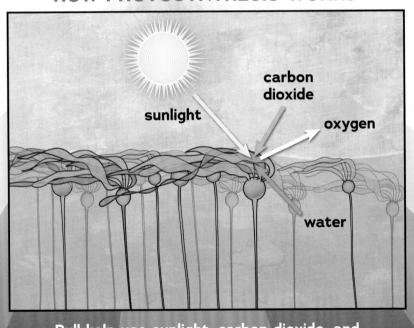

carbon dioxide

sunlight

oxygen

water

Bull kelp use sunlight, carbon dioxide, and water to make their own food.

Plants also make oxygen as they make food. The oxygen goes into the air and water. Animals breathe the oxygen. They breathe out carbon dioxide. Plants use the carbon dioxide to make more food.

Algae

Water contains chemicals called nutrients. Living things need nutrients to grow. Plants get nutrients when they take in water. The nutrients become part of the plants.

Ocean plants make oxygen that animals breathe. Fish use gills to get oxygen from the water.

Algae are plants that float in the water. Most algae are too small to see. But huge numbers of algae grow in the ocean. Algae make the water look green.

Some algae are a kind of plankton. Plankton are living creatures that float and drift in the water. Some plankton are producers. Other plankton are small animals.

Algae are the most important producers on Earth. Algae make most of the oxygen that animals breathe. Ocean animals also eat algae. Algae need sunlight to grow. Sunlight is brighter near the surface of the ocean. So algae grow only near the surface.

Algae cover rocks along this ocean coast.

Large algae called seaweeds also live in the ocean. Most seaweeds grow near the shore. Some seaweeds float on the surface of the ocean.

No algae grow in the deep parts of the ocean. Light cannot reach there. The deep waters are dark. But deepwater animals need algae too. They need the oxygen algae make. They depend on the animals that eat the algae.

Strange-looking creatures live in the deep, dark parts of the ocean. This deep-sea angler feeds on other fish. Those fish eat food that drifts down from the surface.

Chapter 3

OCEAN PLANT EATERS

This northern kelp crab lives and feeds on kelp. What other ocean animals eat plants?

Living things that eat other living things are consumers. *Consume* means "eat." Animals are consumers.

Animals that eat plants are called herbivores. The sun's energy is stored in the plants. When an animal eats plants, it gets the sun's energy. Most ocean herbivores are small. Tiny animal plankton float in the ocean. Many animal plankton feed on algae. Small worms eat algae. So do baby clams and shrimp.

What Eats Algae?

Copepods are also a kind of animal plankton. They look like tiny shrimp. Copepods eat algae. Oysters eat algae too. Oysters take in water. They strain algae out of it. Clams also filter algae from the water.

Snails scrape algae from rocks to eat. Snails also eat kelp. Sea urchins feed on kelp. So do kelp crabs.

THIS IS A COPEPOD. COPEPODS ARE VERY SMALL. THEY ARE NOT MUCH BIGGER THAN THE PERIODS ON THIS PAGE.

Some larger animals eat algae. Green sea turtles graze on algae. Some fish eat algae too. Blue tang eat algae growing on coral reefs. Corals are tiny ocean animals that build stony homes. Over many years, the corals' homes pile up to make a rocky reef. Many ocean plants and animals live in and around coral reefs.

Blue tang swim by a coral reef. The fish feed on algae that grow on the reef.

Chapter 4

OCEAN MEAT EATERS

Most ocean animals eat meat. Meat-eating animals are called carnivores. Carnivores catch and eat other animals. Carnivores depend on plants too. Carnivores get energy by eating animals that have eaten plants.

Octopuses hunt near the ocean floor for other animals to eat. What are animals that eat meat called?

Many ocean animals eat animal plankton. Jellyfish catch plankton in their long, thin tentacles. Sea anemones also catch small animals in their tentacles.

A WHITE-SPOTTED ROSE ANEMONE FEEDS ON A JELLYFISH.

Ocean Hunters

Ocean fish eat other animals. Sea bass eat worms and crabs. They hunt small fish. Bluefish and tuna are fast swimmers. They catch smaller fish to eat. Some sharks eat bluefish and tuna. Sharks also eat octopuses and other large ocean animals.

Octopuses are carnivores. They hunt for crabs. Octopuses eat lobsters too.

A blue shark takes a mouthful of anchovies.

Whales are meat eaters. Some whales eat animal plankton. Right whales eat copepods. Killer whales hunt for fish. They also attack birds and seals.

Seals and sea otters eat fish. Sea otters also feed on sea urchins and crabs. Seabirds also feed on fish. Pelicans dive into the water. They catch fish in their beaks. Gulls and terns catch fish too.

A sea otter bites into a crab.

Omnivores

Some consumers eat both plants and animals. These animals are called omnivores. Damselfish are omnivores. Damselfish eat algae. They also eat animal plankton and small, shrimplike animals.

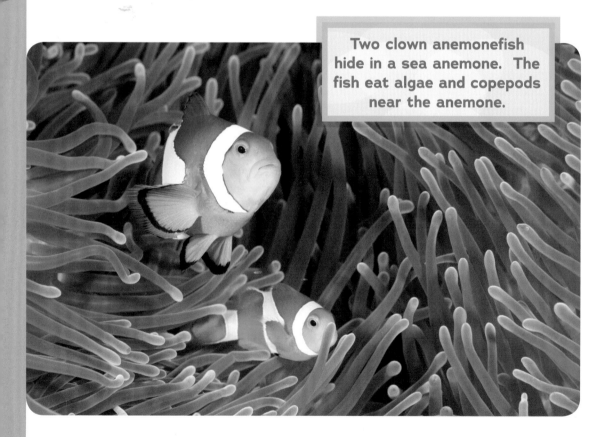

Two clown anemonefish hide in a sea anemone. The fish eat algae and copepods near the anemone.

A school of
herring zooms
through the water.

Some fish gather plankton in their mouths as they swim. These plankton feeders are omnivores. They gather both plant and animal plankton to eat. Herring and anchovies swim in large groups. These fish swim with their mouths open. They feed on the plankton they catch.

Mole crabs are omnivores. Mole crabs burrow in wet sand. They filter the water in the sand for plankton to eat.

Chapter 5

OCEAN DECOMPOSERS

All living things die. When plants or animals die, they decay. They break down into nutrients. Living things called decomposers help dead things decay. Decomposers feed on dead creatures.

A dead fish sinks to the bottom of the ocean. What will happen to its body?

Nature's Recyclers

Decomposers are nature's recyclers. They help break down dead plants and animals. Dead creatures sink to the bottom of the ocean. Decomposers feed on them. The dead plants and animals slowly become part of the mud. Nutrients from them go back into the water. Then other living things can use the nutrients again.

Something has killed a large number of fish in this part of the ocean. Decomposers will break down the bodies into nutrients for algae and other ocean plants.

Decomposers are very important. Without them, the ocean would be full of dead plants and animals. Then no new plants could grow. Animals would run out of food.

Some ocean animals are scavengers. They find and eat the bodies of dead animals. Some sharks feed on dead animals floating on the surface of the water. Crabs and lobsters live on the ocean floor. They eat dead animals that sink to the bottom.

This lobster found a meal on the ocean floor.

Bacteria

Sea cucumbers live near the ocean floor. They hold on to rocks or crawl along the sand. Sea cucumbers swallow sand. They eat bits of dead things in the sand.

Bacteria are the ocean's most important decomposers. Billions of tiny bacteria live in the water. Billions more live in the mud. Bacteria feed on dead creatures in the water and mud. They break down the creatures into nutrients.

This dead sea turtle is decomposing on the ocean floor. Crabs and other animals will pick away at the body. Tiny bacteria will break down what is left.

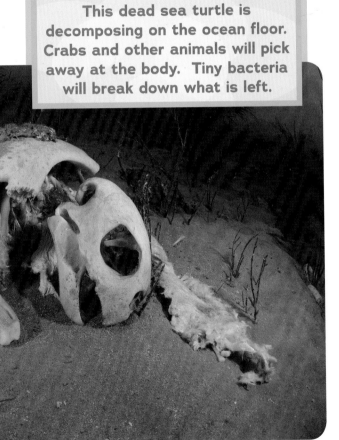

Chapter 6

PEOPLE AND THE OCEAN

The ocean is very important to people. We eat food from the ocean. We travel across the ocean and live by its shores. Ocean algae make the oxygen we breathe.

A diver swims near a coral reef. Why do people enjoy the ocean?

The ocean affects our climate. Ocean water holds heat. The water flows to cooler parts of the world. The water carries heat with it. The ocean makes the weather warmer in those places. Cold ocean water flows to other places on Earth. The water cools the land there.

THE OCEAN TAKES IN AND STORES THE SUN'S HEAT. THE OCEAN CARRIES THAT HEAT TO OTHER PLACES ON EARTH.

Ports and Fishing

People build cities near the ocean. These cities have ports. Big ships come into the ports. These ships carry products across the ocean. Ocean ports let people trade with faraway places.

This port is near New York City. The ships carry products across the Atlantic Ocean.

People and their activities can harm ocean animals. There are lots of fish in the ocean. People catch fish to eat. Sometimes people catch too many fish from one place. These fish die out. Ocean animals that eat those fish must find other food.

These fishers caught herring. People eat the fish and their eggs. Companies also use herring to make fish oils and animal feed.

Wastewater pours into the ocean.

Extra Nutrients

People can harm ocean water too. People put fertilizer on lawns or farmland. Fertilizer has nutrients. It helps plants grow. Sewage also has nutrients. Sewage is waste and water carried away in sewers and drains. Rain washes fertilizer and sewage into rivers. The rivers flow into the ocean. The nutrients from the land enter the ocean.

The extra nutrients can make algae grow too fast. That makes the water cloudy. Then underwater plants cannot get enough light. They may die.

Algae use the nutrients. Then the algae die. When they decay, bacteria feed on them. The extra bacteria use up oxygen in the water. Animals in the water may not be able to get enough oxygen to breathe.

These fish died because they could not get enough oxygen from the water. Bacteria used up the oxygen.

Protecting the Ocean

The ocean is huge. But it is still harmed if we use it as a place to get rid of waste. Sea life dies if we dump waste in the ocean. People can work to keep fertilizer and sewage out of the ocean. We can also change the way we catch fish so that we don't take too many.

Trash on the ocean's shore can get washed into the water. Picking up the trash helps keep the ocean clean.

People love to visit the ocean. We go to the beach. We swim and catch fish. But the ocean is more important than that. It gives us food. It gives us oxygen. It keeps our climate mild. We must take good care of the ocean environment.

TWO CHILDREN RUN
ALONG AN OCEAN SHORE.

Glossary

algae: water plants that use sunlight to make food. Some algae are tiny. Other algae, such as seaweeds, are large.

bacteria: tiny living things made of just one cell. Bacteria can be seen only under a microscope.

carnivore: an animal that eats meat

consumer: a living thing that eats other living things. Animals are consumers.

decay: to break down

decomposer: a living thing that feeds on dead plants and animals and breaks them down into nutrients

environment: a place where a creature lives. An ocean environment includes the air, water, sand or mud, weather, plants, and animals in a place.

food chain: the way energy moves from the sun to a plant, then to a plant eater, then to a meat eater, and finally to a decomposer

food web: many food chains connected together. A food web shows how all living things in a place need one another for food.

herbivore: an animal that eats plants

nutrient: a chemical that living things need to grow

omnivore: an animal that eats both plants and animals

photosynthesis: the way green plants use energy from sunlight to make their own food from carbon dioxide and water

plankton: small plants and animals that float in the ocean

producer: a living thing that makes its own food. Plants are producers.

scavenger: an animal that eats dead plants and animals

Learn More about Oceans and Food Webs

Books

Johnson, Rebecca L. *Journey into the Deep: Discovering New Ocean Creatures*. Minneapolis: Millbrook Press, 2011. Travel deep into the ocean and learn about fascinating sea creatures scientists have discovered in the last ten years.

Kapchinske, Pam. *Hey Diddle Diddle: A Food Chain Tale*. Mount Pleasant, SC: Sylvan Dell Publishing, 2011. Sing along with this lighthearted romp while you learn about many different food chains in one ecosystem.

Wojahn, Rebecca Hogue, and Donald Wojahn. *A Coral Reef Food Chain: A Who-Eats-What Adventure in the Caribbean Sea*. Minneapolis: Lerner Publications Company, 2010. What you choose to eat shapes your fate in this fun, interactive story about food chains.

Websites

Dive and Discover
http://www.divediscover.whoi.edu
Join marine scientists on expeditions to different parts of the ocean. See videos and photos and read interviews and stories about life at sea.

EcoKids: Chain Reaction
http://www.ecokids.ca/pub/eco_info/topics/frogs/chain_reaction/index.cfm
Put together a food chain and learn why every living thing involved is important.

The Food Chain
http://www.sheppardsoftware.com/content/animals/kidscorner/foodchain/foodchain.htm
Play interactive games to help you learn more about what makes up a food chain and how it works.

Expand learning beyond the printed book. Download free, complementary educational resources for this book from our website, www.lerneresource.com.

Index

Photo Acknowledgments

The images in this book are used with the permission of: Zeke Smith, pp. 4, 13; NASA/GSFC/ NOAA/USGS, p. 5; © Reinhard Dirscherl/Visuals Unlimited, Inc., pp. 6, 28; © Laura Westlund/ Independent Picture Service, p. 7; © Francois Gohier/Photo Researchers, Inc., p. 8; © David Wrobel/ Visuals Unlimited, Inc., pp. 9, 21, 23; © Juniors/SuperStock, p. 10; © Alexsvirid/Dreamstime.com, p. 11; © iStockphoto.com/Island Effects, p. 12; © iStockphoto.com/Stephan Kerkhofs, p. 14; © Biletskiy/ Dreamstime.com, p. 15; © Doug Perrine/Alamy, p. 16; © Minden Pictures/SuperStock, pp. 17, 20; © blickwinkel/Hecker/Alamy, p. 18; © Comstock Images/Getty Images, p. 19; © Richard Herrmann/ Visuals Unlimited, Inc., p. 22; © Vladoskan/Dreamstime.com, p. 24; © Aldo Brando/Stone/Getty Images, p. 25; © Paul Nicklen/National Geographic/Getty Images, p. 26; © Paolo Curto/The Image Bank/Getty Images, p. 27; © NHPA/SuperStock, p. 29; © iStockphoto.com/Rainer von Brandis, p. 30; © Galyna Andrushko/Shutterstock.com, p. 31; © fotog/Getty Images, p. 32; © Nordic Photos/ SuperStock, p. 33; © David Woodfall/Stone/Getty Images, p. 34; © Leroy Simon/Visuals Unlimited, Inc., p. 35; © jf/Cultura/Getty Images, p. 36; © iStockphoto.com/omgimages, p. 37.

Front cover: © Mark Webster/Oxford Scientific/Getty Images.

Main body text set in Adrianna Regular 14/20
Typeface provided by Chank